God's Wisdom for Your Worries

To...

From...

"True wisdom and real power belong to God;
from him we learn how to live,
and also what to live for."

Job 12:13
(The Message)

When you need wisdom

If any of you need wisdom, you should ask God,
and it will be given to you.
God is generous and won't correct you for asking.

James 1:5
(Contemporary English Version)

Cling to wisdom –
she will protect you.
Love her –
she will guard you.

Proverbs 4:6
(The Living Bible)

I would have you learn this great fact:
that a life of doing right is the wisest life there is.
If you live that kind of life,
you'll not limp or stumble as you run.

Proverbs 4:11–12
(The Living Bible)

Photos: Lizzy Standbrook, Summer Garden

When you are worn out by worries

Hear my prayer, O God;
don't turn away from my plea!
Listen to me and answer me;
I am worn out by my worries.

Psalm 55:1-2
(Good News Translation)

"Can any one of you by worrying add a
single hour to your life?"

Matthew 6:27
(New International Version)

God cares for you,
so turn all your worries over to him.

1 Peter 5:7
(Contemporary English Version)

Photo: Lizzy Standbrook, Sleepy George

When you are waiting and worrying

"...I alone know the plans
I have for you,

plans to bring you prosperity
and not disaster,

plans to bring about
the future you hope for."

Jeremiah 29:11
(Good News Translation)

When you are anxious

"If only my anguish could be weighed
and all my misery be placed on the scales!
It would surely outweigh the sand of the seas..."

Job 6:2-3
(New International Version)

I sought the Lord, and He answered me;
he delivered me from all my fears.

Psalm 34:4
(New International Version)

God is our refuge and strength,
an ever-present help in trouble.

Psalm 46:1
(New International Version)

When you feel insecure...

...I pray

that Christ will be more
and more at home
in your hearts,
living within you as you trust in him.

May your roots go down deep into
the soil of God's marvellous love;

and may you be able to feel and
understand... how long, how wide,
how deep, and how high his love
really is; and to experience this love
for yourselves...

Ephesians 3:17-19
(The Living Bible)

When you don't know which way to go

The LORD says,
"I will guide you along the best pathway for your life.
I will advise you and watch over you."
Psalm 32:8
(New Living Translation)

Take the first step in faith. You don't have to see the whole staircase. Just take the first step.

Martin Luther King
American pastor, 1929–1968

Lord of the journey, I commit my life and my way to you.

When you feel out of your depth

When you are *weak* –
then you are *strong*.
His grace is enough.
Let Him take over.

"My grace is sufficient for you,
for my **power** is made **perfect** in **weakness**."

2 Corinthians 12:9
(New International Version)

Photo: Lizzy Standbrook, Courtney at the Wheel

When you are afraid

I trembled and shuddered;
my whole body shook with fear.

Job 4:14
(Good News Translation)

GOD's angel sets up a circle of protection
around us while we pray.

Psalm 34:7
(The Message)

For he will order his angels to protect you
wherever you go.

Psalm 91:11
(New Living Translation)

Photo: Virginia Duhanes, Flames

When you have been hurt or let down

"My relatives have gone away;
my closest friends have forgotten me."

Job 19:14

Even my best friend, the one I trusted completely,
the one who shared my food, has turned against me.

Psalm 41:9
(New Living Translation)

There are friends who pretend to be friends,
but there is a friend who sticks closer
than a *brother.*

Proverbs 18:24
(World English Bible)

When you are under pressure

We are merely moving shadows,
and all our busy rushing ends in nothing.

Psalm 39:6
(New Living Translation)

He lets me rest in green meadows;
he leads me beside peaceful streams.
He renews my strength.

Psalm 23:2-3
(New Living Translation)

Then, because so many people were coming and going that they did not even have a chance to eat, he said to them, "Come with me by yourselves to a quiet place and get some rest."

Mark 6:31
(New International Version)

Lord, when life is fast and I am getting breathless, help me to feel your presence in the pressures.

Eddie Askew
Christian writer and artist, 1927–2007

When your worries seem huge,
and God seems far away

How long will you forget me, Lord? Forever?
How long will you look the other way
when I am in need?

Psalm 13:1
(The Living Bible)

Be still, and know that I am God!

Psalm 46:10
(New Living Translation)

I believe
in the sun even when it is not shining.
I believe in love even when I cannot feel it.
I believe in God even when
he is silent.

(Found on the wall of a Jewish hiding place during the Holocaust.)

When you feel alone or forgotten

I am lonely and troubled.
Show that you care and have pity on me.
My awful worries keep growing.
Rescue me from sadness.

Psalm 25:16–17
(Contemporary English Version)

The LORD

will work out his plans for my life
– for your faithful love,
O LORD, endures forever.
Don't abandon me, for

you made me.

Psalm 138:8
(New Living Translation)

When temptation is overwhelming

My guilt overwhelms me —
it is a burden too heavy to bear.

Psalm 38:4
(New Living Translation)

And God is faithful. He will not allow the
temptation to be more than you can stand.
When you are tempted, he will show you
a way out so that you can endure.

1 Corinthians 10:13
(New Living Translation)

Consider it pure joy, my brothers and
sisters, whenever you face trials of
many kinds, because you know that
the testing of your faith
produces perseverance.

James 1:2-3
(New International Version)

Photo: Lizzy Standbrook, The High Cross, Ffald-y-Brenin

When you are grieving...

... I am convinced that neither

death nor life...

... neither angels nor demons,
neither the present
nor the future,
nor any powers,
nor anything else
in all creation,
will be able to separate us
from the love of God
that is in

*Christ Jesus
our Lord.*

Romans 8:38-39
(New International Version)

When you fail, when you fall

Humble yourselves before the Lord,
and He will lift you up.

James 4:10
(New International Version)

And the God of all grace... will himself restore you
and make you strong, firm and steadfast.

1 Peter 5:10
(New International Version)

Father, thank you

that your faithfulness is new every morning.
When I stumble and fall remind me to stop
worrying and give the situation

to you.

When you are worried about money

What do you need today?
Energy to make it through the day? Finances? Wisdom?
You have two alternatives: panic or pray.

Rick Warren
Author of *The Purpose Driven Life* © 2002, www.zondervan.com

Don't worry **about anything,** but in all your prayers
ask God for what you need, **always asking him**
with a thankful heart.

Philippians 4:6

Look at the birds in the sky!
They don't plant or harvest.
They don't even store
grain in barns.
Yet your Father in heaven
takes care of them.
Aren't you worth more than birds?

Matthew 6:26
(Contemporary English Version)

When you feel depressed

I have seen it all, and everything is just as senseless as chasing the wind.

Ecclesiastes 1:14
(Contemporary English Version)

"Don't be dejected and sad,
for the joy of the LORD is your strength!"

Nehemiah 8:10
(New Living Translation)

You lead me to streams of peaceful water,
and you refresh my life.

Psalm 23:2-3
(Contemporary English Version)

Photo: Lizzy Standbrook, Hippopotamus

When doubts surround you

I cry out day and night, but you don't answer,
and I can never rest.

Psalm 22:2
(Contemporary English Version)

He reached down from on high and took hold
of me; he drew me out of deep waters...
He brought me out into a spacious place;
he rescued me because he delighted in me.

Psalm 18:16 & 19
(New International Version)

Doubts can be the *bridge* to faith. Take time to work through your doubts and when you're finally across the river you'll find your faith standing on firm ground.

When you have lost hope

Why am I so sad?
Why am I so troubled?
I will put my hope in God,
and once again I will praise him,
my saviour and my God.

Psalm 43:5
(Good News Translation)

May the God of hope fill you with all joy and
peace as you trust in him,
so that you may overflow with hope by the
power of the Holy Spirit.

Romans 15:13
(New International Version)

Jesus said...
"I have come as a light to shine in this dark world,
so that all who put their trust in me will no longer
remain in the dark."

John 12:46
(New Living Translation)

When you feel tired
and weary

God arms me with strength,
and he makes my way perfect.
He makes me as surefooted as a deer,
enabling me to stand on mountain heights.

Psalm 18:32-33
(New Living Translation)

When you have health worries

God knows what you are going through
and he cares.

Let all that I am praise the LORD;
may I never forget the good things he does for me.
He forgives all my sins
and heals all my diseases...
He fills my life with good things.
My youth is renewed like the eagle's!

Psalm 103:2-3,5
(New Living Translation)

"Let the beloved of the LORD rest secure in him,
for he shields him all day long,
and the one the LORD loves rests between his shoulders."

Deuteronomy 33:12
(New International Version)

Give all your worries to God, he can handle them

"If you'll hold on to me for dear life," says GOD,
"I'll get you out of any trouble.
I'll give you the best of care
if you'll only get to know and trust me.
Call me and I'll answer, be at your side in bad times..."

Psalm 91:14-16
(The Message)